YOUR CRIB, MY QIBLA

African
POETRY
BOOK SERIES

Series editor: Kwame Dawes

YOUR CRIB, MY QIBLA

Saddiq Dzukogi

University of Nebraska Press / Lincoln

Acknowledgments for the use of copyrighted
material appear on page x, which constitutes
an extension of the copyright page.

The African Poetry Book Series has been made
possible through the generosity of philanthropists
Laura and Robert F. X. Sillerman, whose
contributions have facilitated the establishment
and operation of the African Poetry Book Fund.

Library of Congress Cataloging-in-Publication Data
Names: Dzukogi, Saddiq M., author.
Title: Your crib, my qibla / Saddiq Dzukogi.
Description: Lincoln: University of Nebraska
Press, [2021] | Series: African poetry book series |
Identifiers: LCCN 2020031224
ISBN 9781496225771 (paperback)
ISBN 9781496225788 (epub)
ISBN 9781496225795 (mobi)
ISBN 9781496225801 (pdf)
Subjects: LCGFT: Poetry.
Classification: LCC PR9387.9.D985
Y68 2021 | DDC 821/.92—dc23
LC record available at https://lccn.loc.gov/2020031224

Set in Garamond Premier by Laura Buis.
Designed by N. Putens.

For Baha

21 November 2016 to 12 December 2017

These are poems born out of grief and the celebration of our beloved daughter Baha, who we lost twenty-one days after her first birthday. In writing these poems I feel like I am holding her in my hands. She is alive as grief, alive as memory, alive as song.

CONTENTS

ACKNOWLEDGMENTS

Immense love to my wife, Mirah, the mother of my children, whose strength I lend each time I step into the world. My deep gratitude to Kwame Dawes, for being a light that never dims, through the bleakest of nights, and for mentoring me to be a better poet and person, for the warm hugs and for generous advice and guidance as he untiringly worked with me through many versions of this book. I'll love to say a big thank-you, friends, Leslie Ann Mcilroy for her heart and for being a friend and genuine glimmer of what that word *friendship* is. Angel Garcia, Olufunke, Jamaica, Katie Henson, David Ishaya Osu, Hussain Ahmed, Henk Rossouw, Tsitsi Ella Jaji, Wale Owoade, thank you for pushing me and these poems to be better versions of ourselves. Also, gratitude to Ted Kooser, a compassionate teacher and mentor, for encouraging me to do the work needed to put this book together. A special thank-you to Chris Abani, Matthew Shenoda, and the entire editorial board of the African Poetry Book Series, for their unflagging support and for paving the way that my own journey is a lot less tasking than theirs. Immense gratitude to Auntie Lorna, for being a loving mother to me and my family. To BM Dzukogi, the late Musa Hamisu, Zulaihat Musa, Khadijat Sakiwa, my children's grandparents, I say thank you. I will also like to thank the entire English Department of the University of Nebraska–Lincoln, for providing me the space to grow myself and my poems.

Finally, Baha, thank you for coming, however brief your stay was, there is a light that will endure many lifetimes, in my heart, because of that coming.

All thanks to the editors of the following publications, in which these poems, sometimes under different titles and versions, originally appeared:
  The Account: "Inner Songs" and "Still-Life"
  ANMLY: "Strain" and "Revival"
  Bird Feast: "Observations"
  BOAAT Press: "Cave"
  Boxcar Poetry Review: "Measurable Weight"
  Cosmonauts Avenue: "Flower's Tenderness"
  DIAGRAM: "Burial Sheet" and "Quenching"
  Dunes Review: "Ribbons" and "My Son Asks if I Miss My Daughter"
  Ellipsis Literature & Art: "Unexpressed Grief"
  Glass Poetry: "Waterlog"
  Grist: "Measuring the Length of Grief by the Length of a River"
  Gulfcoast: "Marshmallow"
  Jalada Africa: "Seismic"
  The Journal: "Chibi"
  The Laurel Review: "Memories by the Sea"
  The McNeese Review: "Wineglass"
  More in Time: A Tribute to Ted Kooser: "Song to a Birdwoman"
  Obsidian: "Shahada" and "Janazah"
  Orison Anthology: "Cave"
  Oxford Poetry: "One Year After" and "Internment"
  Oxford Review of Books: "A Song in the Mouth of a Ghost"
  Poetry Daily: "Quenching"
  Rhino: "Aubade"
  Spillway: "The Conceit of Shadows"
  Stay Thirsty Poets, Vol. 2: "Aubade"
  Vassar: "Elegy"
  Verity La: "A Kind of Burden"
  Verity La Anthology of Best Works: "A Kind of Burden"

YOUR CRIB, MY QIBLA

I | YOUR CRIB

Wineglass

When your mother found strands of your hair
hung up in the teeth of your comb,
your father squirreled them into a wineglass.
It bites him hard that your life happened

like an hourglass with only a handful of sand—
this split to the seam of his body, a split
of darkness that won't kill him but squeezes
adrenaline into his veins, so he lives

through the pain of your absence. He's not all right
to speak. His voice rims with bereavement,
and he wants to sing by your grave, child,
now that birds blow songs through

the window—counts sadness on the prayer beads
necklaced around his collar. *If he had known the sky*
would inhale you out of him so quickly,
he would have stayed with your toes forever

in his hands. Your face is still everywhere,
even in the places he is not looking.
He presses a deep kiss on your grave,
on your forehead.

Hands, cloudy from rubbing the grave,
as if on your tender skin.
The distance he feels is more

than the four hundred kilometers that often stands
between you. He will travel this far
to hold you against the moon.
They say you are like his reflection

pulled out of the mirror he stares into.
To pull you out he plunges his hand
inside himself and pulls.

Song to a Birdwoman

Her mother, labor blood still trickling down her legs
passes her to him, cradled in the towel of her arms,
the hospital waiting hall full of the baby's face, a hand
glass holding the shrunken reflection of her
mother as of a nursling. The mirror goes back
in time. The moment she sets foot in his palm,
a river of light dispels the night that subdues
the leaves of the neem tree pillared outside.
A wind comes to him and love crosses a strip
of wood, doorsill, windowpane, through
every barricade and bears his body to the night's and
earth's brightest star. The night of her birth,
he sleeps in the car, in the silence of the neem tree
overhead with leaves watered
by the same luring silence. He hungers for her cry,
her first-time voice, but she opens her eyes instead,
eyes like she has taken them from her mother's sockets.
Tears furrow his bones, rinse his bones
until he turns pure steed, ready to saddle her on his back.
Eyes dazzle with the excitement of fatherhood,
light falls to that moment as his hair
glints beside the light clenched into a pulpy fist.
This is to the girl rescinding the pitch dark
so what remains is the value of light, such eternal
seed bearing, same forever through all that makes him
insufficient. He was born into solitariness

that shreds. The moment he began as her father
he roved and only knew his flaxen-flower,
and solemn prayer that he sees her sung up as a birdwoman
gliding into every space that fills the sky.

Internment

Your mother's breasts swell with milk.

She cups each in her hands
as she delicately squeezes the warm milk
through puffed-up nipples into a polythene bag,
paces into the yard, roots her knees to the earth,
hands muddied as she digs the spot

where she entombs the milk there
in the place you used to play with your brother.
She leans back, looks into an open sky
like one who has found a way
of sending the milk across to you.

Burial Sheet

He comes to sing, lying on the cold floor,
a fragment of his sadness, where
his mother washes his daughter's inert body.
His mouth is where pallbearers drop
condolences like toffee. He smells the floor
to sense her scent. Hones his anguish
into a sharp nail and presses it
hard against his neck. The day
she died, he lay in the cordial slice
of an afternoon below the dome of the house
humming over an empty crib.
His mother wrapped her in a burial sheet. Miles apart
from that site, he wants to die so he can drag the child back
into her mother's arms. It's a respite
to even think he could achieve such a Godly act.
In his daughter's absence, he is surprised that
her light glows more. Stuffs her napkin into his back
pocket. He can't sit when his grandmother
offers him a chair. He arrived late to the interment.
Washed down to his toes with the news. He misses
his child like she has been dead
for a thousand years. The feeling ripples her face
against his mind, and his mind feels like a mind
of darkness. He walks through a bridge
beyond himself, within his small beginnings,
with the countless realms of sadness
between him and the light she keeps inside his heart.

So Much Memory

Now he answers to everything that reminds him of her,
a crib rocking, a circle of faces
crowing at him. He can neither leave his eyes open
nor shut them. Splits the night
walking between two cornfields, striding
like he's going for the thing he'll never find.
See how he runs his hands over his body,
how his skin peels. After a night of crying,
he can feel her limbs in his palms,
versified, nothing made of flesh;
nothing made of bone. He opens his mind
and lets the leaves be his skin
and lets a song fall inside another song:
it mimics his daughter's voice.

Scarf

His *prayer like wool too worn out to warm* his bare feet,
a frigid climate of grief climbs up his toes until legs quiver
in response. He wishes grief were a cloth he could take off.

Unsure if your ghostly body will show itself
in the deserted corners of the house, he peers into every void.

He runs into the woods to see what rattles
the half-opened leaves of the twigs.

He can't explain just how sacred an act
sniffing your clothes has become.

Your mother says your body has molded
into a seraph's—your hair, ribboned with a piece of her scarf,
says anyone who hears
the voice of God cannot be heard.

But at the hillock of the woods,
he hears your voice like a swarm of locusts
glazing the trees. He footslogs all the way
into himself to find out how long it will take
to carry his heart out of this rack of grief.

All the body parts you laid hands on
feel like scars. In his prayers
he says he wants to see you, even if as a suggestion, a mark
on tree bark. The more he meditates, the more
he expects you to appear anywhere—
even in your brother's teacup.

The Fruit Tree

She comes as a wind with her brother's ball
and places it into his palm, the earth
spinning on its orbit as his bare body
levitates, her eyes deep
and shiny with the ardor of stars,
and he asks what juice comes from the fruits
of the placenta tree? She whispers the recipe
and he holds it in his body, the river
that meets the roots and only speaks
through the open eyes of leaves.
He stays in the company of all her toys
as he remembers how she clutches each
by the tail. It is her way of keeping in touch.
Under the tree, he's in the bathhouse of memory.
She enters his skin
and lays hands on bones. He wonders
how to feel a ghost's touch
despite the dirt of loss in his eyes—
he walks into the fallow of grief—the sharp ends
of the grass cut into skin—
cracks him open for scavengers.
Now the fruit is thick as milk
and now it seeds—bubble-
like with all the things he has lost as a father:
her soft fingers on his chin, her eyes
that open all the hidden chapters
of his body. The ghost is a wine.
He drinks this last memory.

A Nimble Darkness

Six days after she died, he stays the day
on the balcony where she first kissed his cheek,
a vague face weighs a nimble darkness,
reaches him with absolving hands eager to consume.

He measures the time it will take to fix his mind,
swallows an island too big for his mouth,
bones chewed by the water

of her loss. The darkness drenches his skin,
a deluge against a city. His bones make several songs,
a deep sea that breathes into him—his grief.

He is confined,
70 percent roaring water,
30 percent its darkness,

a bedrock extreme that wedges the sun.
Wonders why the prayer her mother passes into
his mouth doesn't dispel the darkness,
the floorboard of a swelling dark-being
climbing back from places where his scream is loudest.

His psalm is refusing to grow in his heart.
The pigeons no longer come to his windowpane,
just bats and dead butterflies.

He Didn't Get to Say Goodbye

He glances at your mother's grief, spread like a republic
too vast to be seen from above a cliff. Harmattan
blows its curb grasses. He had no idea
that you would transform into a glut of daisies across
every climate he strides. He knows you mean to care for him;
you must have tried hard to tell him you wouldn't stay
bound up in the circle of a clock.

When he recognized you as his daughter, you, the resin
released into every wound that appears
in his universe—He felt rescued.
There isn't a single printed photograph of you in the house.

Every night is a night of grieving where light and darkness
seem to shade each other, a stretch of sorrow sucks the color
out of everything. Even a blossoming garden appears in black and white.

He doesn't want to offend you, but
he still has important things to say,
things he knows the dead won't hear.

The House Held by Chaos

He returns one night to her anger.
She crawls away from his open arms like a boat
rowing into sea-space, so fast she scraped her knees
to pass a message into a body craving cordiality.
He needs no more than that now, seeing her,
even if she's to reject his arms. The house she left
is held together by chaos, it clatters into a darkness
that sieves through till it grows a hand to strangle him.
It is true he blames everything on her departure.
After she died, all the days he was away in kaduna
began to hawk him deeper into regret.
The whole toil of providing her a living
quarters decomposes before him.
It is unsayable what echoes inside of him,
like some word that has already been said.
There is no space in his voice for anything
other than sorrow. It clings like a shadow,
something he cannot step out of,
a house, a masjid. It temples in his heart.
He's cursed into constant worship.
He does not blame himself enough because
he's living inside people who love him,
who treat him with courtesy,
who sing of how her death shouldn't push him
into a dark room.

Marshmallow

Today Baha is not dead; she is six years old,
forcing marshmallows into his mouth.
Says I'm grown enough to feed you, Abba,
with the future, that's what she calls him,
just like her brother. He forces
depraved cumin flowers back
into their seeds. The delight is that he has
pulled his shadows back into his skin
to salve his wounds, and all the times
he sat crying are erased—able to sidestep
the void just as he wished. She is at his feet
playing with his toes, as though they are
an extension of her toys—
His image of love pronounced in the way
she holds on to his big toe, rubbing her finger
across its nail—Grandmother says whatever he willed
would become. He didn't understand until now how
over the years, he sat quietly and watched her grow
inside of him, unknotting regret
until it becomes loose, like a house
made of smoke-bricks. Whenever a brick
is laid, the wind dispels it—and
the house exists only in blueprint.
He is traveling inside grandfather's clock,
arrives at the garden where Baha
serves him honeycomb
in her mother's tea cup.
Thirty-thousand leaves are supplicating to nature

and the air is pure—He picks apples
for his daughter. His cupped palms
not an empty cave—a bowl of water
for his child. She is drinking into the future—
a transient hope deep inside,
found by the girl in his body—
the real version of himself. He thinks:
six years ago, Baha went inside of me
to keep her company and we kept
growing, like two trees in a sterile field, the dream
of marshmallows and my daughter still alive.

Enigma

When he arrived at the cemetery
the rusty gate was in his hands, locked.
He jumped over the fence, ran all the way
to get to his daughter,
who waits for him in her grave.
All the graves are unmarked. Someone
said he will find the one where a dry tree
branch slants over with much enigma.
Because fetish people go in to steal
a corpse, the police stopped him from leaving.
That day, they made the cemetery
into a cell and asked his father-in-law
to post the bail. The second time he visited,
he did so with her mother, held outside,
only able to touch her child through him.
Like other women, she's not allowed inside.
Her mother waves her pain at him,
her face in her palms. However
she can, she passes on signals
to give to Baha. Her fingers
twitch in prayer. The water gathers.
This is not a fair accounting
of her tightly knit grief. Her eyes overflow.
He can never get to comfort her
by the grave of their child. To be able to lay
her hands where her child rests,

she pulls the good from his heart.
He draws fables and hands them over.
Heaven knows the unseen,
so, he borrows prayers from the sky.

Palms

He can see her eyes, light jazzes inside
the lamp holders, in the spaces she leaves behind.
He says maybe his daughter is there in the night
as splintered moonlight. This is his own face
carved. Her mother shows him her own hands
says it reminds her of the girl
who suckled her breast. He touches the darkness
below her mother's reflection.
It does not cling to his fingers
where memories sprout as fingernails. They lurk
on bulwarks like alligators, when his soul comes halved
in a haul, he hears the rupturing of his muscles,
her navel cord needling back from her body
into his stomach. Palms pulsate from fielding the body
that left. He wishes his hand could grow a mouth.
Wishes that mouth would tell him how her rind
gathers the energy to nurse his universe.

He wishes he could hold his daughter.
The palm is a ritual site of holding.
In that palm he keeps massaging—expecting the oomph
of the child that once lay there to mold out,
spiraling up from the little lines
pitched in hands. Every morning the routine of seeing
those palms continues, and her mother asks,
"in her absence, what do I hold in these hands?"

Shoes

He watches as the leaves conceal her footprints
all the way through the boulevard

that steered her away. On the second night
after she left, her brother came to him,

hands like a shoe rack packed with her footwear.
Said *Baha forgot to go with her shoes.*

Her soles map his preferred place of grief.
He makes holy all the shoes her feet entered.

He holds her leopard-skinned plimsolls,
the ones she wore on her birthday.

He wants to unweave her braided hair.
Her voice still gales in his head. When he closes his eyes,

he sees her chase after her grandmother's cat.
She says when children pass away, they turn

into stars. His eyes remain inside the sky—
for figments outside dreams—

He wants to know how long it will take
to pull her out of all the spaces

where she exited. He should stop
buying shoes she'll never wear.

Measurable Weight

In your hand, Baha, your father stands
watching the world. Each cock crows the path
until it blossoms. He thinks of the unwanted roses
living alone in grandmother's backyard. A river
roots a flower, a cave cradles a sacred place,
bares a cider orchard, flower spots.
When she named your brother heaven's flower,
and you the river of the world, spouting water
around the household, all season long,
your mother was trying to weave things
into a skylight—Your color, tranquil
like seabirds—He knows you are different.
In your palm the contrived air of the house,
deep silence and calm—your voice inside the walls,
echoing, echoing through every corridor still.
He feels if he had been home with you,
you would still be here. Believe him,
he hasn't mentioned any of this in his prayers,
but in the recesses between words.
He keeps your memory buried in his vacant spaces,
even if they harm his body.
You have his permission to follow
your differences—a throb, a flute, a measurable
sound that flies to where there is no sky
and what his eyes can cull from this deep ravine.

The Gown

He looked at his gown, felt like ripping it off.
In the way it heavies on skin,
the whole weight of the loss that comes,
something inside the body, a primordial
black hole gores out his soul. The cloth
like rarefied muscles ruptures
bones, a giant snake
squeezing his edging into an opening.

He resents this gown. It is hot inside
almost as if dressed in a furnace
and his skin streaked with lines of throbs—
throbs of pain—his heart will remain the same,
never will it hike down this agony.

He wishes he could lion through this grief
without the enfeeblement that comes
from wearing a little leaf around his waist
and sit on ears and not hear anything,
anyone, gurgles on the ache
to crack deeper until it grasps
where the daisy lies. He envies his grief,
dreams to go into himself and lie
down close to his child.
He wants to rip his cloth,
skin, and see her robed in a plaid gown,
her hair ponytailed, raising her leg
by pulling her toes.

His heart is a train packed
with commuters, the quietness
that rises among all that noise drowns him,
her death is inside their voices,
inside his gown, inside all the things
he finds dithering.

This Web

In the washroom he finds the moon
lurking in the mirror, a spider
at the edge of the sink, and a nightingale

who fills the dark edges of the room with a voice
that scuttles his soul into its corners.
Why is it there, out of place?

He's caught in the spider's land of interlacing thorns,
yells back at everything that has a voice,

even the crickets singing into a forlorn night.
How does he descend into the light
that startles a vanishing flower back to life,

even before life began? The whole of death
feels horrible, everything decayed
to ashes in his palms. His life diminishes,

even before a garden breeds the nightingale.
This web, a place that leaves him
wanting.

Shattered

A raven's song echoes against a wall
where the bark of a tree is a rough marble-face, a place
to put his tongue so it says what needs to be heard. Nothing
is sustained inside his mouth but stories, stories
that deepen everything looking for light
inside the raven's mouth, steeped in the dense waters of morning.
Sadness runs like a white horse deep
into the gravity human eyes have never touched
until it scratches the place where a soul is weak,
where a flaw is most visible, where
light fills his bones until light
and darkness collapse into each other.
The mind turns into a hem,
a black hole where escape is a prayer
that is never answered.
Prayer is now the dark
side of light, a night
so impenetrable, heavy
with a silence that tears the neighborhood,
his skin, his entire body.

A Kind of Burden

Silence like emptiness is reciprocal
when you speak against a wall,

knowing is a kind of burden.
A hummingbird whistles

down his throat. After
a hard swallow,

his daughter's name morphs
into a world inside a hummingbird's abdomen, cracks

the margins that constrict pain
inside the body.

Learning about Constellations

Today Baha is not dead; she is twelve years old,
sits beside a flower vase, presses her thumb to the clay.
Her heart buds into a magnificent sun,
waterfalls its warmth all over her satin face.
Taller than all her classmates,
in the corner she leans her head to white paper,
carves moons out of her notebook,
while other children
sit and listen to the teacher. The class
is learning about constellations.
She takes colors off a flower, folds it to her skin.
A chameleon gathering quotes from leaves,
she questions daisies, reveals all suggestions
when he stares into her eyes.
Baha grabs a speck of darkness,
molds it into a moth and places it in the darkest point
in his eyes. He sits close to his daughter in the yard—
joins her and the moths. Baha is not dead—
she is walking her way into myth, a world
of new constellations where buried milk
nourishes the placenta to heal
his broken bones, broken eggshell of his heart, mend
each back together with the energy of a clock
that never stops moving backward.

Elegy

Night milk, the clandestine opening of what will stay closed,
eyes when all else has gone cold,
return to the overnight finding of peace,
black milk, black milk hidden out of view——
still the mirror on a wall gives him back his swollen eyelids
and mud-hands fill the peepholes in dream—
drink a homemade wine, camel piss, black milk,
piss milk forced into his throat to wipe clean sorrow—
black night and a rotten yolk broken out of its eggshell.
Drink the morning sink into his knuckles,
drink the morning prayer for a shadow—
neither dead nor alive, crammed with the silence of black-ash.
There he asks the many questions of fire, of wind,
and his daughter's hair is a glint slipping away.
Black night and the valley-spaces between fingers,
till the hair rumps to the end of a road,
nestled on the heap-head of a figment——
Child, child, there isn't anything to see, *black milk of morning,*
they drink you at night, a story of the blind, lacerating—
a story of a child cooked in her mother's milk,
the language of the dead he learns with milk,
your mother's nipple, where hope hangs
in tiny milk-spots
Black milk of morning, they drink you at night—
the city drowning in your mother's milk-sack,
drowning, drowning, drowning.

Quenching

It is to be hoped that a tree
will let its leaves rot
into earth as nourishment;

He is searching
for a piece of ribbon.

Finds it hanging on the door-hedge.
Stares long until he hears
a voice rising

from the knotted edges of the silk.
And he enters into a conversation
like a racehorse released into fire.

Your songs endure

inside his bones.
They will nourish the loneliness—
yours and his.

Back to Life

All the memories of his child
gather into a culture of tears,
a hulking shadow, grinning
in the corners of their small apartment.
Baha's face pads as a moth
against the leaden lights of his thoughts.
Every single time he closes his eyes,
he pictures each drop of tears swelling
with Janna inside. Opens his eyes
to the umbrage,
befogging every grieving step.
He still senses her through skin,
the spaces where she rests her head
and falls asleep, the weight of love blankets
his body. His fingers, the pulsing toy
she craves to put in her mouth.
Wonders if memory is enough
to bring Baha fully back to life,
or if it's safer that she continues,
secreted in his body.

Ba Shi, Ba Shi

Daybreak subsists in his heart,
creeps into every corner of the city,
dislodges the songs of every household—
nothing manifests on his tongue—

He resolves to tread the grove
and sense what nascent flowers do.

The pattern holds all the stories together,
a banquet, a field of humid beach stems,
his body burning in grief.

Ba shi, ba shi, give it to him.

In the mirror his face is old, his sadness
evident in the curves and intersections,
where wrinkle-lines cross over each other
and he asks what is this ancient planet
of streaks and planes where the dead gather.

You appear to everyone close to him in dream, but not him.
Still, he is rehearsing what to say—

The Conceit of Shadows

The universe asks what fruit was born
when he buried your placenta. Through the river
of under-earth, where your mother's lamp
smothers the glow—an inaudible copse of trees
awakened—Hope gleams.
He's not complaining
about the flowers that shed their colors.
What do you see now that light
is withdrawn from your pupils, stripping
shadows of their conceit? He can't follow
the dark road of this new light, that sits halfway
through the corridor of his grief,
a dove attempting flight with clipped wings—
stones hurled from all directions—
there is nothing. The moment,
the buried milk—the buried placenta,
the ghost of a child's body frozen
as death contents in the small world
of membranes, that lack shadows.
You are heaven—depths sculpted
of the finest hands and intentions—
flowers and rivers, swim under his affliction—
into the sublimating rapture itself—
this is the fruit that is borne when kernels
go down into a cesspit.

Strain

He shifted his body from the fragment of the world,
where all the atoms of your departure are sustained—
your grave, his agony, the polythene bag
brimming with breast milk.

He can't break away from the things that remind him you are gone.
The napkin they used to wipe your face after you ate,
he tucked into his bag
after your funeral. He stretches, swallowing all the screams
in the earth, with limbs still devoted to memory.
The night is solid on his skin—his stomach
growls in a broken voice.

Trapped in a loop he can bear no more,
the brink, where the world becomes custodial—with barbwires
that rend its nooks into small rooms he cannot enter.

So long in the dark, pupils adjust to a new gloom,
and his hands become eyes—leading him
through the walls to a doorknob.

It's been a month since you left.
He wishes he could step into your mother's prayer
and swap it with the harvest of his silence.

Window

Today Baha is not dead; she is listening to the flame
in the stove as it cooks her favorite meal,
the food teetering inside the pot.
She can do this language of understanding when
it is cooked by chewing the rice to feel if it's gone soft.
She leans back against the wall in the silence that washes
the kitchen after her cell phone rang and she drops
the mackerel in the simmering oil. Her mother's voice rings
a presence that touches their ears, and they listen.

Is Memory in Her Brother's Body?

for Rayhan—

Baha leaps in excitement,
even if it's just her shadow in him.
Theirs is an unrelenting story of a brother
loving his sister through the void.
The father remembers always waking to the sound
of their giggles, that is how he knew the sun
had risen. He'd make a wall of pillows
to keep her from falling off the cradle.
They conversed in secret, in a tongue held up
in water. Their choice game was when she sought him
out, hidden behind the bookshelf
she saw him, and her eyes glittered
starry with trinkets. He'd forgot his lips
on her forehead when he kissed it.
They didn't know her smile
glowed in the dark, until he showed them with glee—
the father calls her name and he answered. What remains
is a blind hope that she will return
home to the prayers poured into him;
knowing he is a pitcher that will not contain.

Dates

He offered a sacrifice
on the day she was born, planted date trees
and prayed she grows to eat from them.

When he first saw her crawl, in his head
he saw a hand stretched out to give him water, a ritual
cleansing of a body for the future.

The life of his child, a tree that delivers hollow pods,
swallows promises into its branches. Imagine Baha's hair

thickening into a dusky brook
as she walks, holding the hands of two children
whose faces slave in the river of her curls.

Ribbons

The best parts of his face and the best parts
of her mother's collided in hers.
In her eyes he felt his being.
A head full of pink ribbons;
when he kisses her cheek; a fresh plum
packed with the scent of pine leaves.

Now he pulls together the songs from her bones.
Holds his daughter's body and watches
it grow in his palms. The moor
takes possession of empty caves,
and into a room through the window.

Revival

The dancer walks between the dead and the living
while the courtyard stills in a seethe of bees, a chimera.

He's dizzy from this funeral dance of revival.

Against a foul smell, he kneads his bones
back into childhood. Grandmother says children possess

eyes that see everything, even the empty spaces under the dome
of a haunted masjid. They reveal the deeper understanding of loneliness.

If he goes on and says something from the flawless abundance of God,
birds will come to the window wheedling grief out of his eyes.

Cave

He went to the masjid,
found all those who have gone in to pray
under a tree turned into shoes,
heels worn, worked and covered with dust. The earth
is inheritable with the pain of seeing the dead
weave silence into a path
out of this world.

He manipulates memory, so she is in two places,
dead in the makabarta and alive
in his heart.

No healing exists
beneath the ground. We suffer
only the weight of the living, and a sea of longings
below the darkness of deep water.
In six days, the wound of loss will reopen and bleed
and clot and bleed and clot
until he can only pretend healing
or smile in a way that it is not in the heart
the next time he walks into the masjid
knowing a bullet
drags him closer to God than to prayers.

Sufficient

She poked him out of a dream, the third time
in a row, a dream about attending
his daughter's funeral. He wants to swallow
the god that let his child slip away, wants to feel it
slide down his throat and digest like the bone
he once swallowed by mistake.

You are holding it the wrong way,
her mother said, in a voice sodden with tears—
the piece from grandmother's Quran
that says Allah is sufficient—verses laid inside
a lamb's peel, dried, stitched, and given its own skin.
Grandmother said it would eat his insatiable grief
until something good grows from it—a butterfly,
a thing bred out of a crawling ugliness.

This makes sense but not for long.
He beats his heel on a drum. The sound is a funeral
hymn he never got to hold in his mouth.

He doesn't know how this grief appears
in writing, a thing language cannot decipher.

Months have passed, but
whenever the sand he fetched from the heap
on her grave touches his palm, he cries
harder than the last time. Still, he kept that part of earth
the way his mother keeps her jewelries
teetering at the edge of a wardrobe.

Chibi

In the long grass he sat watching the picture
of his daughter, tallied all the memories evoked
of her, saying his name until a light came on
in his eyes. The memories played like a playlist
of all his favorite songs. Tinged her face
with the stem of a mango tree he planted
close to where he buried her chibi. As he sulked
in that climate of heartache,
mosquitoes congregate and mistake his afro
for a marshland. Light shines brightest
in dark places, he wanted to see like a bat
what was before him, a child long buried.
Wanted to hear her cry, like the time
grandmother heated a piece
out of a broken clay pot, pressed it on her navel
for seven days until the string fell.
When his mother said through memories,
he can have his daughter back. He conjured more memories
and bade her to ride each like a horse,
until she arrives. Crickets sang on top of their voices,
sang and sang, until theirs was a voice,
inside his veins. Memory is a shell where time is ductile,
where it draws him in, until the present and past
became tactile in his body.

Shahada

Today Baha is not dead—Her tears reveal deep love
for him. He prays his daughter's hand turns

the sponge that would wash his corpse—
the rite of passage pressed into her forehead,

a prayer mark from birth—
in this dream state he's dying. She passes

on the shahada into his mouth after her tongue
formed the words, a scrum of flowers

beside her knees, hands lift toward the sky
as if she is trying to open a doorway,

his body slips into the bowl, as he imbibes the water
she spit Quran verses into.

He floats when she scours qursiyu
against his eyes. Today Baha is not dead,

she is the shield that repeals a surfeit of darkness
from owning his body, an eel out of mud-water.

Seismic

In the market-square he leans against the tower
as the world passes by. A hole,
the extent of two palms fisted together
in his chest. Often, he prays to perish into silence,
the silence of nights removed from a prayer's
ointment, to lay the wound bare.
Each time he turns his face toward the east
and presses his forehead to the ground,
he sees his daughter beside God, in the eyes of
people, in the eyes of the world, as a witness
to the sprouting of meadows. See how the earth proceeds,
nourishes the ground after a drought. When he faces the moon
and says he's the pitch, the earth mends back
its plates that shift from quake to quake.

The Breadth of a Butterfly

On Friday, her mother called to say *Baha is ill*.
Saturday, he was back in Minna, where
hospitals are places of hostilities. Hours before the doctor

came, nurses with their swollen eyes
looked for Baha's collapsed veins,
her eyes like light bulbs right after a power-cut

flicker back into darkness.
She is pale, her mother said. *No madam she is not,*
let us do our job.

But their job is to fail at *doing* their jobs.
Seated on a wooden bench in the waiting hall,
crammed with smell of blood and iodine

aging inside dumpsters, he recites all the prayers
his mother put into his mouth as a child. The cannula
after hours of looking for her veins

now hangs loosely on the side of her brow.
In his hands he transported her from lab to lab
for blood tests, until finally in a ward

they were given a bed. As her cry grew alongside the discomfort
in her body. His worries flock
in the air as he listens, wishing the pain was a pill

he could swallow on her behalf. His butterfly-
child is still colorful but unable to fly.
Because he doesn't like to drown in regrets, he pictures the flower
her mother planted into her hair.

Flower's Tenderness

Bababaa, just the way his daughter says it,
swirling out of her mouth like a bubble gum
balloon, around her loving lips. He listens
climbing into the garden
in her eyes—a word.

He remembers when their smiles went
into each other. She forced her way
into the heart of the world with
tenderness. She took a lantern and dropped it
over the lea of his dark heart.

She is a November rose,
a scent that swells in his room
like light growing over his darkness.
He always comes home to her eyes
bulging as a full moon, pure as zamzam spring.
Says: your eyes Baha, the moon
opened in darkness. Fondles the sound
of all the words she tries on her tongue,
most of the time the words are barely formed,
but he gets her as if the sound is a language.

On the day of her only birthday, she dips
a finger in the cake before she slips
it into his mouth. On her face are the words:
I will care for you. Though she says it without her tongue,
her smile wound into his heart.

Now each time he smiles, holds her in his face,
the outcome of pollination, the flower on a reel,
a color that reflects even in the murkiest of places.
Now he walks without any misgivings
that the dew on grasses is her little presence
and the way she encompasses the field
with poise—that every withered flower
finds its color again.

Memories by the Sea

Imagine a forlorn child; conceive the sun
that rouses the mouth of the universe. Imagine it
disappearing into the throbbing throat of night—
Imagine the dark seams, thick threads that bind voices
to a giant vault of silence. Imagine him rubbing his fingers
across your picture, trying to gloss your lips with words
as you wander off into the horizon.
Imagine your face—still a sky paring down
into his mind, now—imagine the sun
as reverie—and there, by a sea,
he's leaning to fetch a bit of that firmament.
Imagine this, when his mother says your shadow—
its bedlam inside his body—
a seashell swallows the wave back into its depths.
Imagine looking deeply until his reflection convinces you
you can exist as a fraction outside his corneas.
Imagine you're a star   trancing in his thoughts—
Imagine he disposes those thoughts about you,
in more thoughts about you. Imagine each time
you feel like forgetting something about him—even if insignificant,
imagine glaring the blue zenith boarded in a surface
marred by tides—until the memories split apart
by the sea reassemble like a solved puzzle-
picture. How he wishes you imitate that multiplicity
and grow into the right
places that would hold you whole. He hears the night holds
on to your voice like a basket finally able to hold water.
Imagine he presses his feet against wet sand

and slips through a footprint—here's a mystery
close to the shoreline.   A portal—
Here's the distance, the vast sea
between your bodies. Your voice still
a light, wading through the dark—beyond
the troughs of separation. Imagine. Imagine. Imagine
how you'll communicate, from here on—
Grieving is the only way he speaks of nothing.

When He Says Your Name

he utters a thing most beautiful.
This is how you pull him out of the ground,
even as your essence passes out of this world.
He won't forget. Other times he's a mouth
swallowing only your memories, your light
collected in his bones. Every scent that lingers
in your bib, bootees, and teethers—
where you always play with your ribbons:
the frontlines of extraction.

Your crib, his cathedral—
where he kills time doing nothing.
Sometimes when it's difficult to say,
he stuffs his body with grief.
Parents want to be buried
by their children. In the streets he wonders
what it means to attend such a rite.

A Song in the Mouth of a Ghost

This is a time he won't forget—You
pouring your brother's watercolor on the linen
he now holds like a map, a compass that shows
the place you've gone to, drawn in greasepaint,
alive, grown, in a schoolyard playing
with other kids your age. You're 12.
In other images, you're 16, 20, 31, married—
playing with your toes, like you did with his,
your children are fully-fledged,
have children of their own. You're plaiting
the hair of one. A song in the mouth of a ghost,
a gust of wind from a skull below
his wave of remembrance and desire—a stone
carved out of a bigger stone, a grave-wall
opens into a room that misplaced your body,
moved from labyrinth to labyrinth,
until the weight of your passing breaks
a foothold. He remembers your mother
removing chaff from the unhusked rice,
you, playing on the millstone,
ruining your napkin. The same he clenched
in his fist while glancing at your tomb.
This is how you pull him out
of the ground, giving him your hand,
pulling until he falls
into the temple where you've been waiting,
possessed with longing.

Half-Light

He leans on the kitchen counter baking bread,
like he bakes your memories into a language
that never leaves his tongue.
Often, he asks where you are, like he does not know.
Each time he opens his hands to silence,
the way sunflowers open their face to the sun,
he does not feel your warmth like the flowers,
and wonders if his prayers are dregs,
penumbras of what can no longer hold anything.
He tries hard not to say the word *mourning*,
hoping that his ability to hold it unuttered
will alter this reality. Your mother's breasts
milk for you, wait in vain for your mouth.
His body is transfixed in that opening
between half-light and darkness, the cavity
in the lower part of the Grief-face,
the shadow you left behind. Your leaving,
a curdled taste he is forced to swallow.

What Belongs to Him

This is how sorrow holds his mouth
without space. He believes your bones
tell stories the sun cannot
turn to ash. Your love
twinkles below his pillow,
there is no darkness. Always,
when he turns clouded, gives the river
a message; the mist crosses a bridge
peering up to your new world.
Sometimes wishes the whole universe
could explode in his mouth. He remembers
when you trapped a butterfly
beneath your fingers. He'll forever be
in distress. When he's lonely,
he yowls into a hand-mirror
until his reflection leaps out
like it's running from a pack
of wolves. His loneliness scares.
It's evidence he's not going insane.

Aubade

He woke up one morning, sees his son
rubbing thumb over a screensaver,
his sister's face. In his eyes, his son—
the lamentation of a brother.
He imagines the interrogations:
"Mammy, where do we go to when we fall asleep?
Is that where my sister went? Why,
when I put my ear on your stomach, do I hear her
talking to me? What song is sowing
her bones back into your womb?
What is lost in a vale? When I place my finger
on your belly button, can I retrace her existence?
Mammy, when even the familiar can no longer be seen,
and absence becomes a kind of presence,
will you speak in my sister's voice,
a sound found inside your throat, a cry
in a borrowed language from a sister
who best understood my own language,
even within the bounds of my silence?
Mammy, my sister's name
is still the clamor of this melancholy we share
over the dinner no one eats. What else has vanished
into Abba's eyes that dopes the flame of candlelight?
It is dark——a dark that extends
from the broken light bulb
and drags itself into the sinkholes, into the sewers——
there and still here,
an enormous body that panders after
us to every other place we dare to go."

II MY QIBLA

—A Dialogue

She Begins to Speak   *Baha*

I am shimmering behind a wall,
like a flame in a lantern. Hold me

down in your body. Everything
in my life is fragrance;

myrtle, chrysanthemum, freesia.
I want to watch as you plant daffodils

where it aches the most. Turn your heart into
a garden. The place of my rebirth

attracts joy like petals attract insects.
Everything in my life is a flower,

I live inside the smell like a moth
twirling toward the farthest bulb——

Don't despair, it reflects on me.
I am anchored to your feelings.

Inside your body, it spikes when you despair.
I think of all of you in the household,

and quiet down like a seed in an ovule,
quiet like a ghost armed

with knowledge of death
for the first time. I quiet down

like wall flowers growing on
the creepers leaning on me, growing

over me. I keep my shape,
the shape of the dead, that is how

I'm allowed to stay now. I am here but
almost not, that is how ghosts exist,

almost a figment. There is nothing sad,
do not despair in the universe

as a miniscule, for I am here,
more than a memory, when you remember
me, I become whole for a moment,

before cringing back into this form,
absorbed inside a frame, absolve yourself

of the guilt, it is the only way for me
to live. I hear you crave my voice

in your dreams, the thing is, I do not
know how I sound and I'm scared

of speaking in a way that you won't know
it's me. But know that your voice is in

my body, you echo in my bones,
quite loudly, the one dead feels alive.

Speaking to you, I ask too much
from behind this wall.

I want to manifest in ways that convince you
I'm watching the world as it wrinkles, alongside your skin.

I cannot stop, it is my life-source to watch you,
my brother, and mother, it's a joy splattered

over my face like sunlight. My right hand
a torch pointed toward any darkness

that confronts you. When the daffodils grow,
my rebirth is complete. Your grief is empty,

when your pillow dries—put it out there
let sunlight claim its wetness.

I know what you feel, that sadness
keeps me physical in your body,

but you have to let go, it's a monster
bullying me here—I have my mother's hand,

go on and hold her. What else can open
your eyes? My eyes are still

there, and whatever you saw in them
you can see inside my mother's.

There is grief inside, as well,
but it's only by looking that you can

get it out. They won't detonate,
if you stare, taking your eyes off them

is like removing the pins. Do not despair,
my body is stardust across the night sky,

and rays across the day's. Do not let your body
continue as a village, sacked and burned.

Journey Home

Abba

On the road from Kaduna to Minna,
over the phone, I begged my mother
to ask father to wait, not to bury you
in my absence. I cried. I yelled at my aunty
when she asked what difference it would make
whether I was there or not. I just wanted
to see you dead, as if seeing you dead will bring you back.
I poured faith into what is broken
hoping a miracle would justify their action.
In my mind, even though it was going close
to its limits, the car sped in slow motion.

Still-Life

Sometimes memory is more than a knife
cutting moments from my past
into sizes that fit the present. At the edge
of what doesn't seem like paradise,
a myrtle had risen past a skyline.
I still call you Myrtle, abandoning my grief
as I complete your heaven with a fantasy.
I call the shrub your name until it starts
to look like you. Sometimes I am angry:
I know what you've done with my hair
inside a wine glass. We hold onto anything
that reminds us of what we've lost.
As I wake from a dream, lost are
the pearlescent eyes that could see into
tomorrow, could see the myrtle still
stretching its body to reach the horizon.
Memories are a still-life caught in snippets,
framed in a glass, like my hair.
They drag shared moments to my eyes,
where your light touches me and the images
re-form. There we are all together: mother,
my brothers, Farid and Rayhan,
playing hide and seek behind your back.

Janazah

The leaves flap rigorously
when my father's head presses against the earth
during sujud—I hear he managed folding
his shadow by bending his body. Sly—
almost rolled back into the bones.
During your Janazah prayer,

this prayer is a kind of recall—

He speaks through their edges to their weights,
squelching to the sentiment—a tether in my hands
tacky with echoes. What is the purpose
of a body in prayer that only imitates? Purrs its physique
on the spurned lava of grief. Sometimes
this prayer is a mantra that will preserve your bones,
inside a crypt. The prayer rises as it should, like a bird.

The axil of the leaves yellows after the prayer.
My grandmother insists the prayer is a fruit
and the words given to it are seeds
we sow where the land indulges your body.

Observations

Baha

DAYA

Ba, I'm praying
that a hummingbird hands me its ability

to hover and fly backward,
back into a timepiece where I am

myself in a bathwater
you prepared. Startled
that a flower doesn't bloom,

I brood over the idea

of bereavement; a nest
egg of sorrow.
Because there is an ounce of life unfurling inside my tears,

there is no right way
to swallow a sullen pill.
There is a spark

of lifelessness in the bulb

that fails to bloom.
I miss you cleaning
the dirt in my ears,

miss you wiping filth

off my kneecaps,
scrubbing my face
often, so tenderly. Remember the day you put me to sleep

on grandmother's mat?
Everything I need
now is inside the threadbare

blankets you wrapped me in,

because here, my body is a fleabag
where loneliness governs
like a dictator.

BIYU

From the past, Ba,
dying is like moving into a future,
past the street bursting with voices
of the people you know

I am a girl who looks
like her father . . .

UKU

What do I know of a prayer, other than it's a place
where my knees root the ground and palms
curve toward God like a child
waiting to drink from his body?

Because prayers often beget silence,
I am in communion with the half-cleaved side
of my melancholy.

My mouth wads the puzzle in the air,
where I imagine your body pillowing mine
on the heels of your hands.

HUDU

Ba, when I close my eyes,
we are looking the moon in the eye,
the perfect place to dream into. Our bones
gleaming in its dim lights.

Mother once dropped in my ears
these words; a fantasy comes true
if imagined thoroughly.

BIYAR
I hear stars cracking.

Perhaps,
you are the most tragic victim
of my fantasy.

From where I stand,
it's easier to pull the earth
closer to my forehead

than to wait for my prayers
to be answered.

SHIDA

I am lacing your hair into a rope of desire;

a collection of things
beyond one's reach.

Measuring the Length of Grief
by the Length of a River

Abba

In the sovereignty of night, I relive
the days of being your father,
I court the urge of sliding into a dream,
indulging that fantasy of fatherhood—

listening to your heartbeat
I once woke up the world with my excitement.
And if this yearning could now wake you up,
once you wake, the world you find will be a bit more

impaired than the one you left,
and me swallowed in the great rust of mourning,
where everybody whose lives you've touched
has earplugs to shut down themselves

from one another.
Child, my mother says your body shortens
the distance between God and me—a bridge

sprawled from my doorstep into paradise. Perhaps it's true.
Every day I weep in her presence
she presses those words into every corner
of my ears until a smile appears on my face.

And then she crumbles
into her own tears as if the smile on my face
was a big wound that scars my attempts at happiness.
Each time I think about you now, I go into the bathroom

to lean against the mirror and cry, most times
the mirror feels like your body,
sometimes like a ghost or a light of illusion
along a forsaken river. Sometimes I think

your memory is a sky crumbling onto its own
clouds, and the blue sky reminds me of my mother
and her fiend-strength. I am rooted in
what ruptures, a ghost looking for its body

flayed in internal voyage, a circular track
around a masjid. At the entrance of night,
your body is a bright artifact
hanging on the minaret.

Ummi

Each time you pray, your tongue
wrestles with your teeth to say
the ninety-nine names of a non-talking God
that never answers when catechized
to return the dead, not even
when the names are tattooed behind
his ears as a voice calling a stone-deaf
who seems to say, *I am a bit deaf,*
so you'll have to speak up. If silence were a language
prancing in a hand-carved wood doll,
what words would the world hear? Dear Ummi,
each time sorrow weakens your knees in sujud,
and the prayer you offer, questions
the Composer, instead of admonishing—
there is nothing as beautiful as you
weaving a wreath, in praise of my body.

But because your shadow is alive
with grief, no air can stop your lungs,
from gasping for more air, where
pieces of father's blues levitate like blood
from a skin cut open in space. You're
counting years by the number of family
members that have fallen into the part
of earth only seen when you look
into the moon. What does it mean to be
outside a clock, outside its fingers?

Sometimes I come to the house as a wind
and ring the doorbell. When you open the door,
your body is in my face. I fill my nose
with your smell. If you ask me, no one deserves
more praise than the hands bleeding
of my absence, as they mix playdough for my brother,
or as they construct cardboard papers
into houses no one could live in beside the memory
you stork into making them.

If silence were a language prancing
out of a shadow's mouth, what will be heard
in your muffled prayers, anointed
with a tinge of your ire, I know you often blame yourself,
but death wasn't in your breast milk
nor inside anything you fed me.
You wonder if God hears your voice,
Ummi, I hear you.

Unexpressed Grief

Abba

Twigs lean into the windows of the room that was once mine,
smelling of fresh leaves, fresh like the crushed mangoes
in your mother's juicer. My child, you come as memory,

to settle in my mind,
a quarry you've never visited before.
But the leaves of the mango tree are no longer leaves,
just your hands patting my back. To pull your socks

from your shoes, I hauled the cobwebs that gathered like a crowd.

I do not have words of comfort for your mother when she cries
but we perform wudu
to speak to God. We bow our heads
with the same level of reverence I afford my mother.
We recite the Quran
for the daughter who has not been dead

long enough for the wound
to start healing. My mother says we must grieve
according to the Quran: This means in peace,
without tears or words. But in our grief,
you hear its metal rubbing off my bones.
In the Quran there is a solution to every mystery,
but not for an unexpressed grief.

My Son Asks if I Miss My Daughter

It's an aching beauty
when your brother misses you. Says *a tornado*
swirls inside his water flask. I wonder

what music brews. I am holding back
tears at the dining table
slicing tomatoes on flatbread.

I make out time to seek memories.
The whole room ties up in a foil of grief,
a strong-smelling herb that cures nothing—

He asks if I miss you playing muddy-puddle.
His question compressed like a riddle;
where is my sister? On a chopping board
the onion
isn't enough room. My burning body spills
out onto the pan. I explain
my silence like a hummingbird's throat,
crowded with relics, stardust and ash. I am still.

When he asks about you,
my reply is half in epigrams that hold no sense,

sometimes like prayers
stuck in my throat—a fishbone. His questioning
rattles my heart.
When I close my eyes,

it feels like a ghost is singing
my song, but it fades
when I turn—I wonder
what music brews this massive silence.

At Your Grave I'm Reminded of the Day You Were Born

After subhi, the night wears off
from my eyes as dawn approached
and laid soft fingers on the prayer mat,
by then I could see the position

of my own fingers balled together,
my plea for your safe arrival handed
to God like some gift. Throughout the night,
my prayer bead like a track field

where my thumb runs many laps.
I have learned to interpret the nurse's expression
at intervals, in CM's, the sizes

of your mother's second mouth, widening
enough for an entry. Before going to the mosque,
I placed my ear on the wall
of the delivery room, heard so many baby

cries, wondered which one was you, if at all you were there.
I heard so many women cry out in pain,
one wail swallowing the other, overlapping,
confusing me, which one was your mother's.

The more I heard your mother's moan
the closer I thought you were to coming.
Before I went to pray, out
from her womb, a woman pushed a baby
who refused to let air into its lungs.

Another used up her last breath
to push hers, only halfway.
I inherited my mother's
fear and anxiety, my agitated mind
turned into a river that lost its shape
to an external current. The prayer
I gave to God a collection of words, half spoken,
muffled into each other like the screams
of the laboring women. Back in the hallway,
my body felt as light as my shadow,
and I pondered how you will come, how beautiful
you'll grow. Pedaling back on this memory

like the iridescent wings of a moth, fading
out as I open my palms, from where
it has been caught. After the first rain,
your body has gyred into a tulip.

Where Pain Lives

I woke up one morning
and my shadow seemed like a burning cloth
that no longer fit my body.

Dear child, when you pressed your stomach to the cold tiles,
to take in the energy of earth,
just a few weeks before you died. Your pulse
trudged through that which before long claimed your body.

Where your headstone was, I put a mirror,
each time I come to visit
I see that you live in my face,
the only place you can be found.

I put my hands in a fire—searching for bones—
Grandmother said: when a shadow is on fire
the body catches the flame and transforms
into a figment swallowed by the wind;

the places where the fire has touched,
that is where pain lives.

December   *Baha*

I fail to care for the blessing of time,
as sickness, for months, darns my body.
I mess up the future, surrendering to the idea
of dying young. My gaze in the garden-dust
washes off like the bitterleaf mother uses
to make us soup.

I am always in fraternity with that sickness whose name I do not know
or perhaps the rusty equipment at the hospital
is too old to talk, or too blind to see
the uncertainty in my cells.

Despite the fear rustling with my bones
I am never too weak to cut a future out of my clothes
and I do not fall before my mirror where I see
frozen layers of time—a film vulnerable to color. Often
I try to take my feelings to the stars, and they seem to see me;
I imagine their twinkling as nodding of heads. They are all verbs.
Once I heard one say, a star that knows it would turn into dust
the next day, will still shine on the eve of its explosion.

Maybe writing about absence and inserting
me in the corners of empty rooms will span circles.
Maybe the art you create is not a mistake.
Maybe sorrow will cease to swarm around
like ghosts behind lace curtains. The quickness
of my life has no metaphor, and fear is what
the living feels, while trying to preserve a short life on the beach.

Sometimes memory is a tripwire to a larger sadness,
earth-breasted in the mark of my departure.

Memory serves the present and has no future.
Every weekend mother washes my clothes and spreads them
on washing lines as if I had worn them
and would somehow do so again.

Inner Songs

Abba

When I pray, I place my palms one onto the other,
on my chest, as if to say; it is yours,
God, in a voice, deep as a fissure—
where the things that go in, echo
and create circles like a stone
stirring the face of a river—my prayer is a planetary body,
siphons my energy and gives nothing in return.
What light can stir me through
this hailstorm of darkness? What orchestrates my body
to trust its scrapped knees instead of the feet?

Grief means me, means to keep my body swallowed—
paring down my bones to an idea that cannot flower.
It is a virus strafing my immune system like a rock salt
rubbed at my skin where I have bruises,
until the bruises are stripped into wounds
even my shadows can feel. Barefoot,
at the place where earth ate my daughter's
placenta, seeking to empty my sadness,
the sadness of a body, a body like a house
built on buried bones. I am singing to the ravens
and my sorrow spills on the neighbor's wife.

She is pregnant. Each morning when we meet,
I'd see my sadness in her eyes.
I bridle at a beaming light so much
what I see is just a dark so dark it holds my eyes
for a few seconds after I turn away.

I am fond of your memory,
it's the only room where I walk into
and find you on a mulberry carpet
waiting with sealed lips, a face,
a body, and silence.

Waterlog

When mother whispered "What doesn't kill you—"
I replied, "turns me into a living corpse."

I am the spitting image of my shadow,
a face absorbed into a night, aching

from what has been ripped off. I am fluent
in my silence. What transpires after stars collapse—

what happens if the dead turn into trees
corralled into the passage of time, blathering

about its inadequacy to erase existence.
The agony is a silent war in my body, each time

I open my mouth to speak, inhaling more pain
that jam-packs my lungs like a riot ground.

Come into my foxhole with eyes that see
what others can't. Let's shadow each other.

I will collect the light that leaked into the parching
river. My eyes are a window waterlogged

with tears. I cannot see anything
other than what frightens me. I am living

off my fear. How do I consent to joy? If it's a currency
what can it buy? All I want is to crawl

away from a house built in perpetuity for grief,
with corners spidered with longing, pain,

and tears. My tongue inside
a keyhole cannot unlock the door.

One Year After

Today is a year since the earth
opened its mouth to the size of your body
and swallowed. Like a ghost,

I am learning to walk the earth
without my body—regret, a rosary wrapped around
my wrist leads me away

from the universe's favor. If death is truly everywhere
on earth, where could I have hidden you
from its grasp? Perhaps

behind a star that shines every five hundred years.
The shaft of sorrow, like sunlight
striking the ground where I stand.

God knows that I am not perfect
but I found a pearl in loving you.
Each time in the swelling vapor of love,

I hold you, blended into the rainbow
marking its body
across the skyline. The world stops spinning,

instead a bubble grows over it, and time
cannot exert itself on us.

NOTES

In "Wineglass," "If he had known the sky would inhale you out of him so quickly"
   is a slight variation of a line by Sam Roxas-Chua in his poem "Of Blood and
   Stem."
In the poem "Scarf," the line "prayer like wool too worn out to warm" is by Phillip
   B. Williams in his poem "Witness."
The italicized lines in "Elegy" are lines by Paul Celan from his poem "Death Fugue."
In the poem "When He Says Your Name," the line "how you pull him out of the
   ground" is a paraphrase of a line by Jean Valentine in her poem "In the Library."
In "A Song in the Mouth of a Ghost," the lines "how you pull him out / of the
   ground, giving him your hand" are a paraphrase of two lines by Jean Valentine
   in her poem "In the Library."
In the poem "My Son Asks if I Miss My Daughter," "a foil of grief" is phrase from
   Forest Gander.
"Where Pain Lives" is after Pablo Neruda.
"One Year After" adapts a line by Max Ritvo.

Gabriel Okara: Collected Poems
Gabriel Okara
Edited and with an introduction
by Brenda Marie Osbey

Sacrament of Bodies
Romeo Oriogun

The Kitchen-Dweller's Testimony
Ladan Osman
Foreword by Kwame Dawes

Fuchsia
Mahtem Shiferraw

Your Body Is War
Mahtem Shiferraw
Foreword by Kwame Dawes

In a Language That You Know
Len Verwey

Logotherapy
Mukoma Wa Ngugi

When the Wanderers Come Home
Patricia Jabbeh Wesley

*Seven New Generation African
Poets: A Chapbook Box Set*
Edited by Kwame Dawes
and Chris Abani
(Slapering Hol)

*Eight New-Generation African
Poets: A Chapbook Box Set*
Edited by Kwame Dawes
and Chris Abani
(Akashic Books)

*New-Generation African Poets:
A Chapbook Box Set (Tatu)*
Edited by Kwame Dawes
and Chris Abani
(Akashic Books)

*New-Generation African Poets:
A Chapbook Box Set (Nne)*
Edited by Kwame Dawes
and Chris Abani
(Akashic Books)

*New-Generation African Poets:
A Chapbook Box Set (Tano)*
Edited by Kwame Dawes
and Chris Abani
(Akashic Books)

To order or obtain more information on these or other University of
Nebraska Press titles, visit nebraskapress.unl.edu. For more information
about the African Poetry Book Series, visit africanpoetrybf.unl.edu.